Contents

THE
Bon Appétit
KITCHEN
COLLECTION

Festive Entrées

The Knapp Press
Publishers

Los Angeles

Published by The Knapp Press
5900 Wilshire Boulevard, Los Angeles,
California 90036

Library of Congress Cataloging in Publication
Data
Main entry under title:

Festive entrées.

        (The Bon appétit kitchen collection)
        Includes index.
        1. Cookery (Entrées) I. Series.
TX740.F47 1983   641.8'2   83-13620
ISBN 0-89535-124-2

Printed and bound in the United States of
America

On the cover: *Crown Roast of Pork with
Breaded Cauliflower*

Photograph by Brian Leatart

1

Beef

Standing Rib Roast

6 to 8 servings

- ¾ cup all purpose flour
- 1 teaspoon salt
- ½ teaspoon freshly ground pepper
- 1 tablespoon paprika
- 3 garlic cloves, minced
- 1 3- or 4-rib roast (7½ to 10 pounds), trimmed of excess fat, feather bone and ribs loosened and tied in place

  Horseradish sauce (optional)

Preheat oven to 500°F. Combine flour, salt, pepper, paprika and garlic. Rub roast completely with this mixture. Place roast fat side up in shallow roasting pan. (A rack is not necessary since bones form natural rack.) Insert meat thermometer into thickest part of roast, making sure tip does not touch bone. Sear roast at 500°F for 15 minutes. Reduce heat to 325°F and continue cooking as desired.

To determine roasting time:

- Very rare—15 minutes per pound, or 140°F on thermometer.
- Medium—20 minutes per pound, or 160°F on thermometer.
- Well done—25 minutes per pound, or 170°F on thermometer.

When desired doneness is reached, turn heat off, leave oven door ajar and allow meat to rest 20 minutes; or if oven is needed for another purpose, remove roast and let stand in a warm place near the oven. (This makes carving easier, and fewer juices will run out onto the platter, so the meat will be more succulent.) Cut strings and serve with Horseradish sauce, if desired.

If preparing two roasts, place side by side in 17½ × 12-inch roasting pan.

Roast Beef and Yorkshire Pudding for Two

2 servings

  1   rib of a standing rib roast (about 2½ pounds)

  ½ cup milk
  ½ cup all purpose flour
  1   egg
  ¼ teaspoon salt

  2   tablespoons drippings from roast beef

      Horseradish Cream Sauce (see following recipe)

Preheat oven to 500°F. Place meat in roasting pan fat side up, balanced on the bone. Sear roast at 500°F for 15 minutes, then reduce heat to 325°F and continue roasting as desired (see chart with Standing Rib Roast recipe, page 2).

Meanwhile, combine milk, flour, egg and salt in blender or processor and mix well. Cover and refrigerate 1 hour.

Spoon 1½ teaspoons drippings into each of 4 custard cups. Divide batter evenly among cups. Bake with meat during last 20 minutes of roasting time, then remove meat from oven and tent with foil to keep warm. Reduce oven temperature to 350°F and continue baking pudding until puffed and golden, about 10 to 15 minutes. Carve roast at table. Serve with Yorkshire Pudding and Horseradish Cream Sauce.

Horseradish Cream Sauce

Makes about ½ cup

- 2 tablespoons prepared horseradish
- 1 teaspoon tarragon wine vinegar
- ½ teaspoon sugar
- ½ teaspoon dry mustard
- ¼ cup whipping cream, softly whipped
  Salt and freshly ground pepper

Combine first 4 ingredients in small bowl and blend well. Fold in whipped cream. Taste and season with salt and pepper. Refrigerate until serving time.

Steak Tips with Horseradish Sauce

Perfect party fare—an easy-to-prepare buffet dish with its own tangy sauce. Prepare the meat a day ahead, but don't slice it until the day of the party to ensure juiciness. Sauce can be prepared the night before the party and chilled.

25 servings

    9 large garlic cloves or to taste, minced

    6 to 7 tablespoons oil

    3 2- to 2½-pound triangle tip roasts
Salt and freshly ground pepper

Horseradish Sauce (see following recipe)

Combine garlic and oil. Rub thoroughly into meat and sprinkle generously with salt and pepper. Let roasts stand at room temperature for 2 to 3 hours.

Prepare charcoal grill and preheat oven to 400°F. Grill meat very briefly just to seal in juices. Transfer to rack set in roasting pan and roast to desired doneness, about 45 to 60 minutes for medium rare. Remove from oven and let cool. Wrap in foil and refrigerate overnight. Thinly slice and arrange on platter. Serve with Horseradish Sauce.

Horseradish Sauce

Makes 7 cups

> 4 cups (2 pints) sour cream
> 1 cup prepared horseradish, drained
> 5 slices fresh white bread (crusts trimmed), torn into fine pieces
> 2 cups whipping cream

Combine first 3 ingredients in large bowl and mash with fork to blend well. Whip cream until stiff. Stir ¼ into horseradish mixture to loosen, then gently

fold in remainder. Cover and refrigerate until ready to serve.

Sausage-Stuffed Flank Steak

4 to 6 servings

- ¾ pound Italian sweet sausages (about 4), casings removed
- 1 medium onion, chopped
- 1 medium carrot, diced
- 2 garlic cloves, minced
- 1 medium apple, peeled, cored and chopped
- ½ cup diced green bell pepper

- 2 cups seasoned bread stuffing mix
- 1 egg, lightly beaten
- ½ cup chopped fresh parsley
- ½ cup beef stock
- ¼ cup Madeira
  Salt and freshly ground pepper

- 1 2-pound flank steak, butterflied and *lightly* scored on both sides
  Barbecue sauce

- ½ cup water

Break sausage into small pieces and place in large skillet. Sauté over medium heat about 8 minutes. Remove with slotted spoon and transfer to medium bowl. Add onion, carrot and garlic to drippings in skillet and sauté 4 to 5 minutes. Stir in apple and green pepper and sauté until slightly softened, about 3 to 4 minutes. Remove from heat and add to sausage.

Preheat oven to 350°F. To sausage mixture, add stuffing mix, egg, parsley, stock and Madeira and blend thoroughly. Season to taste with salt and pepper.

Spread mixture on meat, leaving ¼-inch border on all sides. Loosely roll steak lengthwise and secure at intervals with string or skewers. Place in roasting pan seam side down and bake 45 minutes. Brush with barbecue sauce and bake 15 to 30 minutes more, or until meat is tender. Remove to serving platter and keep warm.

Degrease roasting pan and place on burner over medium heat.

Add water and 1 tablespoon barbecue sauce and cook a few minutes, scraping pan to blend in any brown bits. Strain. Slice steak thinly, arrange on platter and pour sauce over.

2

Veal

Tour de Veau

8 servings

- 8 slices veal 3 inches in diameter, ¾ inch thick, cut from rib eye or top sirloin of veal
- 1 cup all purpose flour
- 1 teaspoon sage
- 2 teaspoons dried oregano
- 2 cloves garlic, minced
- 1 tablespoon paprika
- ¼ teaspoon freshly grated nutmeg
- ½ teaspoon salt
- ¼ teaspoon freshly ground pepper

- 3 to 4 tablespoons butter
- 3 to 4 tablespoons olive oil

- 8 slices Eggplant Gratin (see following recipes)

8 slices Broiled Tomatoes
(see following recipes)

8 large mushroom caps

2 cans crescent dinner
rolls

2 egg yolks

2 tablespoons whipping
cream

¼ teaspoon paprika

3 tablespoons grated
Parmesan cheese

24 pitted black olives
Fresh parsley

Trim fat from veal. Combine flour with seasonings. Coat veal slices lightly with seasoned flour. Refrigerate for 1 hour.

In a 12-inch skillet heat the butter and olive oil and sauté veal on both sides until golden. Do not crowd the skillet or the veal will turn gray.

On an ungreased cookie sheet place a slice of veal; cover with a slice of Eggplant Gratin, then a Broiled Tomato slice; top with a raw mushroom cap.

Unroll crescent roll dough one can at a time. Separate eight triangles along perforated lines. Cut off 1½ to 2 inches of dough from base of each triangle; save for decorating. Cut each triangle in half vertically. Each veal tower requires 3 strips. Place point of each strip on top of mushroom, drape it down over tower, and press dough to veal at bottom.

Combine egg yolks, cream and paprika with whisk. Brush egg wash on pastry for browning. Cut extra scraps of dough into small crescents or leaves, press onto dough strips, and paint with egg wash. Dust with Parmesan cheese and refrigerate until ready to bake.

Preheat oven to 350°F. Return veal towers to room temperature. Bake in oven for 15 to 20 minutes, or until pastry is golden. Attach 3 black olives with toothpicks to top of each tower. Serve on bed of parsley.

Eggplant Gratin

- 1 2-pound eggplant, cut into slices 3 inches in diameter and ½ inch thick
- ½ cup mayonnaise
- ¾ cup crushed saltine crackers
- ¾ cup grated Parmesan cheese

Preheat oven to 425°F. Coat both sides of eggplant slices lightly with mayonnaise. Combine crackers and cheese and dip eggplant slices into mixture. Place on greased cookie sheets and bake for 15 minutes. Turn and bake 5 minutes more, or until golden brown.

Broiled Tomatoes

- 4 tablespoons mayonnaise
- 4 tablespoons grated Parmesan cheese
- 4 tablespoons minced and sautéed shallot or green onion (excluding green ends)
- 2 tablespoons minced fresh parlsey
- 2 large tomatoes, cut into slices ½ inch thick

Combine mayonnaise, cheese, shallot and parsley. Spread on tomatoes. Place under pre-heated broiler for 2 to 3 minutes, or until lightly browned.

Veal Cordon Bleu with Mushroom Sauce

4 servings

- 8 thin slices ham or prosciutto
- 8 veal cutlets, pounded thin
- 2 tablespoons grated Romano cheese
- 2 tablespoons grated Parmesan cheese
  All purpose flour
- 1 egg, beaten
- ¾ cup breadcrumbs seasoned with 1 tablespoon grated Parmesan cheese, ¼ teaspoon paprika and dash of salt

- 3 tablespoons butter
- ¼ cup chopped shallot
- ¼ cup chopped green bell pepper
- 1 garlic clove, minced

1 cup sliced fresh
  mushrooms
¼ teaspoon cracked black
  pepper
½ cup cream of
  mushroom soup
¼ cup milk
2 tablespoons dry Marsala

Chopped fresh parsley
(garnish)

Lay 2 slices ham on each of 4
veal cutlets. Sprinkle generously
with Romano and Parmesan
cheeses. Top with remaining
veal and press edges together
tightly to seal. Dredge lightly in
flour. Dip in egg, then roll in seasoned breadcrumbs.

Melt butter in 10-inch skillet over
medium-high heat. Add veal and
sauté until golden, turning once.
Remove from pan and keep
warm. Add shallot, green pepper and garlic to skillet and sauté
until almost tender. Stir in
mushrooms and cracked pepper. Reduce heat, return veal to
skillet and simmer 2 minutes to
heat through, turning once.

Meanwhile, combine mushroom soup and milk in small saucepan and bring just to boiling point, stirring frequently. Remove from heat and stir in Marsala. Add to skillet and continue simmering until sauce reaches desired consistency. Transfer veal to warmed serving platter, spoon sauce over top of meat and garnish with parsley.

Veal Rolls Stuffed with Apples

A salad of hearts of palm, tomatoes and lettuce in a vinaigrette dressing and buttery hot rolls round out this menu.

6 servings

- 6 tablespoons (¾ stick) butter
- 1 onion, finely chopped
- 1 garlic clove, minced
- 1 cup soft bread cubes
- 2 cups peeled, coarsely chopped apple
- 1 teaspoon salt
- ½ teaspoon poultry seasoning

- 12 thin veal scallops

All purpose flour

¾ cup apple cider or juice

2 tablespoons Calvados or applejack

Crab apples or sautéed apple slices (garnish)

Melt 4 tablespoons of the butter in a large skillet and sauté onion, stirring often, until golden. Add garlic, bread cubes, apple, salt and poultry seasoning. Stir over low heat until ingredients are thoroughly mixed.

If the butcher has not already done so, pound veal scallops until very thin. Divide stuffing among veal slices; roll up and secure with toothpicks. Coat veal rolls with flour.

Heat remaining butter in skillet. Brown veal rolls well on all sides. Add cider and Calvados or applejack. Simmer, covered, for 25 to 30 minutes, or until tender. Remove toothpicks and place veal on a heated platter. Spoon sauce over veal and garnish with crab apples or apple slices.

Escalopes de Veau Normande

This delicious dish originated in the province of Normandy, France's apple country. Chicken is equally good prepared the same way. Pasta sprinkled with parsley, and artichoke bottoms filled with carrot puree are perfect accompaniments.

6 servings

- 3 large Golden Delicious apples
- ¼ cup fresh lemon juice

- 12 veal scallops *or* 3 skinned, boned and halved chicken breasts, pounded to ⅜-inch thickness
- 1 teaspoon salt
  Freshly ground pepper
- ½ cup all purpose flour
- ¼ cup (½ stick) butter
- 2 tablespoons oil

- ⅓ cup Calvados or applejack
- 1½ cups whipping cream

Peel and core apples and cut into ½-inch cubes. Place in medium bowl and toss with lemon juice. Set aside.

Sprinkle veal or chicken with salt and pepper and dredge in flour, shaking off excess. Divide butter and oil between 2 heavy 10-inch skillets and place over medium heat. When hot, add veal and sauté until golden brown, about 2 to 3 minutes per side. Transfer meat to heated serving platter and keep warm.

Add undrained apples and Calvados to skillets and cook briefly over medium heat, scraping brown bits and glaze from pans. Combine apple mixture in 1 skillet and cook about 3 minutes. Add cream and continue cooking, stirring frequently, until mixture becomes a rich ivory color. Reduce heat to low and continue cooking, stirring frequently, until liquid has reduced by about half and sauce coats spoon, about 20 minutes. Taste and adjust seasonings if necessary. Spoon over veal and serve immediately.

Côte de Veau Moutarde

6 servings

- 6 tablespoons finely chopped shallot
- 5 tablespoons unsalted butter

- 6 veal loin chops, ¾ inch thick
  All purpose flour
- 3 tablespoons olive oil
  Salt and freshly ground pepper

- 1 cup dry white wine

- ½ cup whipping cream
- 2 heaping teaspoons Dijon mustard

In a small pan, sauté shallot in 2 tablespoons butter until transparent. Set aside.

Wipe surface of veal chops with damp cloth. Coat both sides lightly with flour and shake off excess. In a 12-inch skillet, heat remaining butter and olive oil. When oil and butter are sizzling hot, add chops and sauté quickly until golden brown on both sides. Reduce heat and continue cooking slowly about 10 minutes. Salt and pepper chops, place in au gratin pan or rectangular glass baking dish. Preheat oven to 400°F.

Add wine to skillet in which chops were cooked and stir until it reduces to a syrupy consistency. Pour over chops. Place sautéed shallot around chops. Cover with well-buttered waxed paper and lid of pan. Place in oven for 20 to 30 minutes, or until chops are tender.

Transfer chops to heated platter. Add cream to shallot. Bring to a simmer, add mustard and stir well, but do not allow sauce to simmer again. Return chops to sauce, covering completely. Serve at once.

3

Lamb

Rack of Lamb with Fresh Mint Sauce

4 to 6 servings

- 2 racks of lamb (1¾ to 2 pounds each), well trimmed
- ¼ cup brandy
- ½ teaspoon dried thyme
- ½ teaspoon salt
- ¼ teaspoon freshly ground pepper

  All purpose flour
- 1 egg, lightly beaten with 1 tablespoon half and half
- 1 cup Italian seasoned breadcrumbs

Sauce
- ½ cup olive oil
- ½ cup red wine vinegar

6 to 8 fresh mint leaves
1 teaspoon salt
Freshly ground pepper

Place lamb in large shallow baking dish. Combine brandy, thyme, salt and pepper in small bowl and mix well. Pour over lamb, cover and marinate at least several hours or overnight.

Bring lamb to room temperature. Preheat oven to 450°F. Dip lamb in flour, shaking off excess. Dip in egg mixture and then roll in breadcrumbs to coat evenly. Bake fat side up 30 to 35 minutes, or until top is crusty and golden brown (meat will be medium or medium rare).

While meat is cooking, combine all ingredients for sauce in blender or processor and blend. Pass sauce separately.

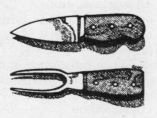

Perfect Roast Leg of Lamb

This glorious dish might be accompanied with baked tomatoes and watercress, and baby lima beans tossed in butter and minced parsley.

6 to 8 servings

- 1 6-pound leg of lamb, fat removed
- 2 garlic cloves, minced
- 1 tablespoon paprika
- 1 tablespoon fresh rosemary or 1½ teaspoons dried
- 2 teaspoons salt
- ½ teaspoon freshly ground pepper

Orange Basting Sauce
- ¼ cup (½ stick) butter
- 1 6-ounce can frozen orange juice concentrate, thawed
- ¼ cup dry red wine

Preheat oven to 350°F. Make 12 slits in meat with point of a paring knife. Combine seasonings and press a little of mixture into each slit.

Insert meat thermometer into thickest part of lamb, being careful not to touch bone. For rare, roast 12 to 15 minutes per pound, or 130° to 135°F on thermometer; for medium, 20 minutes per pound, or 140°F; and for well done, 30 to 35 minutes per pound, or 160°F.

While lamb is roasting, combine sauce ingredients in 1-quart saucepan and simmer uncovered 15 minutes. After lamb has roasted 1 hour, baste frequently with sauce until meat is desired degree of doneness. Place on heated platter and allow to stand in warm place at least 15 minutes before slicing.

To carve, set lamb on its side and slice across the wide end toward the shank. This avoids bone and enables you to cut large pieces of meat. Serve with any remaining sauce.

Lamb Ta Nissia

For a very special dinner party, this delicious presentation of roast saddle of lamb layered with ham and artichoke puree is outstanding. Garnish the platter with lightly sautéed potato balls and individual bundles of crisply cooked asparagus and baby carrots.

6 servings

>   1 4½-pound saddle of lamb
>   6 to 8 grape leaves*

Marinade
>   2 tablespoons fresh lemon juice
>   1 tablespoon olive oil
>   1 large garlic clove, minced
>   1 teaspoon dried thyme
>   1 teaspoon dried oregano

Artichoke Puree
>   1½ tablespoons butter
>   1½ tablespoons all purpose flour
>   ¼ cup finely minced onion

*Available in Greek and Armenian markets.

6 medium to large pureed
   artichoke bottoms, fresh
   or canned
½ cup finely diced
   Armenian string cheese
2 tablespoons Parmesan
   cheese
   Salt and freshly ground
   pepper

6 thin slices prosciutto
1 cup dry red wine,
   warmed

6 mushroom caps, sautéed
   in butter (garnish)

Remove fat, silver skin and flaps
from saddle of lamb. Wash and
dry grape leaves.

Combine ingredients for marinade. Rub lamb with marinade
and cover meat with grape
leaves. Chill overnight.

Melt butter in 2-quart saucepan.
Add flour and blend well. Stir in
onion and cook until lightly
browned. Add artichoke puree,
cheeses and salt and ground
pepper to taste.

Allow meat to come to room
temperature. Preheat oven to
325°F and roast lamb 50 min-

utes. Let stand 10 minutes, then transfer lamb to carving board, reserving juices in pan. Discard grape leaves. Separate each loin from the bone in one piece and cut meat into circles ¾ to 1 inch thick. Spread each slice with some of puree and sliced prosciutto. Reassemble loins, tying slices securely in place. Return meat to roasting pan. Add wine and continue roasting, basting frequently with pan juices, 15 to 20 minutes, or until heated to serving temperature.

Transfer meat to heated serving platter. Remove strings. Skim fat from pan juices; strain juices over meat. Garnish top of meat with mushroom caps.

A 4½- to 5-pound leg of lamb may be substituted for the saddle. Follow the same roasting method, but double recipe for artichoke puree and use twice as much prosciutto. Slice the leg into pieces about ½ inch thick, discarding bone, and form a long loaf with meat and fillings.

Champagne Lamb Chops

2 to 4 servings

4 loin lamb chops, about 2 inches thick
½ bottle Champagne
1 teaspoon garlic powder
Salt

Place all ingredients in baking dish. Marinate 45 minutes or overnight. Preheat oven to 350°F. Drain meat. Bake until cooked as desired, about 35 to 45 minutes for medium.

4

Pork

Crown Roast of Pork with Breaded Cauliflower, Grilled Tomatoes and Sauce Morilles

8 to 10 servings

    1 6- to 8-pound pork loin, frenched and formed into crown

    6 strips fresh side pork or pork back fat

  ¼ cup (½ stick) butter

    1 cup fine dry breadcrumbs
        Salt and freshly ground pepper

    1 medium cauliflower

    1 medium cauliflower, broken into florets

5 ripe tomatoes, cored and
halved horizontally
2½ teaspoons butter
1 sprig fresh rosemary,
oregano or parsley,
chopped
Salt and freshly ground
pepper

Sauce Morilles

¼ cup (½ stick) butter
12 to 15 dried morels,
soaked in cold water
until soft, rinsed
thoroughly, drained and
finely chopped
2 cups rich brown stock
or beef bouillon
2 tablespoons cornstarch
2 tablespoons Cognac

Watercress (garnish)

Preheat oven to 325°F. Cover tips
of pork bones with pieces of aluminum foil to prevent burning.
Wrap pork strips around meat
to retain moistness. Transfer
pork to roasting pan and cook
35 minutes per pound.

Meanwhile, melt butter in small
skillet over medium heat. Stir in
breadcrumbs and cook 3 to 4

minutes. Season with salt and pepper to taste.

About 15 minutes before roast is ready, add whole cauliflower to large saucepan half filled with boiling salted water. Let cook 5 minutes. Add cauliflower florets and continue cooking until crisp-tender, about 9 to 10 minutes. Drain well. Transfer roast to serving platter. Place whole cauliflower in center of roast and florets around base. Pat reserved breadcrumbs over top of whole cauliflower. Freeze juices in roasting pan or other shallow container for 10 minutes; discard fat.

Increase oven temperature to 400°F. Arrange tomato halves in shallow baking dish. Dot each with ¼ teaspoon butter and sprinkle with rosemary, oregano or parsley. Season with salt and pepper. Bake until tomatoes are soft but still hold their shape, about 12 minutes. Arrange tomatoes on platter between cauliflower florets. Turn off oven. When temperature is reduced, return roast to oven to keep warm until serving.

For sauce, melt ¼ cup butter in medium saucepan over medium-high heat. Add morels and sauté about 2 to 3 minutes. Set aside. Add brown stock or bouillon and cornstarch to reserved pan juices. Place over medium-high heat and cook, scraping up any browned bits. Reduce heat and let simmer until thickened. Stir in Cognac and morels and heat through. Transfer to heated sauceboat.

Arrange watercress between tomatoes and cauliflower florets. Serve roast immediately with warm sauce.

Pork Chops and Sautéed Apples

6 servings

> 6 large pork chops, about 1 inch thick
> Salt
>
> 1 cup firmly packed brown sugar
> ⅔ cup crème de cassis *or* Calvados or applejack
> ½ cup apple juice or cider
> 2 large red cooking apples

(Rome Beauty, McIntosh,
Northern Spy, etc.)
1 tablespoon butter
¼ cup dry white wine
½ cup chopped pistachios
¼ cup chopped preserved
ginger

Preheat oven to 350°F. Place
chops in ovenproof skillet and
sear over high heat on both
sides. Sprinkle with salt to taste.

Combine sugar, liqueur and apple juice in small saucepan and
place over medium-high heat.
Cook, stirring constantly, about
2 minutes, or until sauce is
smooth and well blended. Spoon
over chops and bake uncovered
until tender, about 25 to 30
minutes.

Cut apples into thick rings. Melt
butter in small skillet over medium heat and add apples. Pour
in wine and cook until apples
are tender but still hold shape.
Arrange chops in overlapping
pattern on one end of heated
platter. Pour sauce over and
sprinkle with nuts. Arrange apple rings on other end of platter
and fill centers with ginger. Serve
immediately.

Braised Ham with Madeira Cream Sauce

The French often prefer to braise ham rather than bake it. The braising liquid also provides the base for a variety of sauces. This one depends on its own vegetables for thickening and is smoothed by a bit of cream and enhanced with Madeira.

6 to 8 servings

   3 tablespoons butter
   ½ cup chopped onion
   ½ cup chopped carrot
   ¼ cup chopped celery
   ½ teaspoon dried thyme

   ½ mildly cured, precooked ham (about 4 to 6 pounds)
   1 cup dry white wine
   3 cups chicken stock
   3 cups beef stock
   1 bouquet garni (3 or 4 sprigs parsley, 1 large bay leaf, 3 shallots, tied in cheesecloth)

   ¼ cup whipping cream
   2 tablespoons Madeira

Arrowroot (optional)

Fresh watercress
(garnish)

Preheat oven to 350°F. Melt butter in large pot or Dutch oven large enough to hold ham. Add onion, carrot, celery and thyme and cook over medium heat until limp and lightly colored.

Place ham, fat side up, on vegetable mixture and pour wine and stocks around it. The liquid should reach halfway up the ham. If it doesn't, pour in additional stock. Add bouquet garni and bring the liquid to a boil on top of stove. Cover casserole, place in preheated oven and cook, basting every 15 minutes with braising liquid, until it has reached an internal temperature of 130°F (being sure, again, that you are working with a precooked ham—if not, it will have to cook until it is 160°F).

When ham is done, remove from braising liquid and keep warm. With a slotted spoon, remove vegetables from braising liquid and place them in a blender. Carefully skim fat from the liquid and strain 2 cups of liquid into a saucepan. Boil until it has been reduced to 1 cup. Add reduced liquid to vegetables in the blender and whirl. Return this mixture to a saucepan and place over medium heat.

When mixture is thoroughly heated but not boiling, stir in cream and Madeira to make sauce. Season to taste with salt and pepper. For thicker sauce, stir in small amount of arrowroot mixed with water until sauce has desired consistency.

To serve, carve the ham into thin slices and arrange on a platter. Spread each slice with some sauce and decorate platter with bouquets of fresh watercress.

5

Poultry

Chicken

Clay-Pot Chinese Chicken

4 servings

- 3 wafer-thin slices fresh ginger (about 1½ inches long)
- 2 tablespoons peanut or vegetable oil
- ¼ pound mushrooms, thinly sliced
- 5 scallions, cut into 2-inch lengths (tops included)

- 2 cups chicken stock
- 3 tablespoons soy sauce
- 3 to 4 tablespoons Sherry
- 2 tablespoons sugar

1 small roasting chicken
   (about 3½ pounds)
1 teaspoon salt

1 tablespoon cornstarch
   mixed with 2 tablespoons
   water

Watercress and fringed
scallions (garnish)

Preheat oven to 350°F. If covered
clay pot is used, soak it in water
for at least 30 minutes and drain
before using. Sauté ginger slices
in oil for two minutes. Add
mushrooms and scallions and
sauté over high heat for two
minutes more. Remove from
heat and let cool.

Meanwhile, mix together stock,
soy sauce, Sherry and sugar.

Rub chicken inside and out with
salt and fill with the cooled scallion mixture. Close cavity and
tie legs together. Place in clay pot
and pour chicken stock mixture
over. Cover and place in oven for
40 minutes, or until chicken is
tender and done. Transfer to
heated serving plate and keep
warm. Stir together the cornstarch mixture and ¾ cup of the

pot liquids. Cook over medium heat, stirring until slightly thickened. Pour over chicken. Garnish with watercress and scallion fringes.

Spinach-and-Cheese-Stuffed Chicken

This flavorful stuffing is placed under the skin of the breast, resulting in a very plump bird with unusually moist and tender white meat.

4 to 6 servings

- 1 3- to 3½-pound whole chicken, rinsed and patted dry
- 1 pound fresh spinach, stems removed
- ½ cup (1 stick) butter, softened
- ⅓ cup ricotta cheese
- ⅓ cup grated Swiss or Gruyère cheese
- ⅓ cup freshly grated Parmesan or Romano cheese
- 1 egg
- ⅛ to ¼ teaspoon freshly grated nutmeg

Salt and freshly ground
pepper

2 tablespoons olive oil or
softened butter
Paprika

½ teaspoon dried oregano

¼ teaspoon dried thyme

¼ teaspoon marjoram

Turn chicken breast side down.
To remove backbone, cut along
entire 'ength of bone ¼ inch
from center on each side. Discard bone. Turn breast side up
and push down with hands to
flatten chicken slightly.

Cook spinach in 5- to 6-quart
saucepan or Dutch oven until
wilted. Cool, then squeeze out
all excess moisture by placing in
paper or cloth towel and wring-
ing dry. Chop by hand or in food
processor. Combine with butter,
cheeses and egg and mix well.
Add nutmeg and salt and pepper to taste.

Starting at top of chicken breast,
loosen and lift skin with fingers
to create a pocket reaching almost to other end of chicken. *Be
very careful not to tear skin.*

Stuff pocket with spinach mixture. Place piece of aluminum foil around opening, tucking securely to prevent skin from drying and curling.

Oil baking dish or roasting pan. Preheat oven to 375°F. Combine oil with enough paprika to give a rosy color. Combine oregano, thyme and marjoram. Coat chicken with oil, then sprinkle both sides with herb mixture. Tuck wings under body of chicken. Bake about 1 hour, or until chicken is golden brown and tender, basting frequently with pan juices. If breast browns too quickly, tent loosely with foil. Remove foil and cut chicken into serving pieces, making sure each portion has some of the stuffing.

Stuffing may be prepared 1 day ahead. Refrigerate until ready to stuff and roast chicken.

Breast of Chicken à l'Archiduc

8 servings

8 7- to 8-ounce chicken breast halves, skinned and boned

2 tablespoons (¼ stick) butter
½ pound mushrooms, sliced
⅔ cup (about 3 ounces) shredded boiled ham
1 tablespoon dry Sherry
1 teaspoon fresh lemon juice
1 teaspoon fresh tarragon or ½ teaspoon dried
1 small garlic clove, minced
2 cups (about 8 ounces) grated Swiss cheese
   Salt and freshly ground pepper

   All purpose flour
¼ cup (½ stick) butter
2 tablespoons Cognac or brandy

1 teaspoon tomato paste
1 teaspoon Dijon mustard

   3 tablespoons all purpose
     flour
1¼ cups chicken stock
   1 cup whipping cream
   2 tablespoons dry white
     wine
   1 tablespoon dry Sherry
   ½ teaspoon freshly ground
     white pepper

   ¼ cup (½ stick) butter
   8 large mushroom caps,
     fluted
   8 artichoke bottoms
   ½ cup grated Gruyère
     cheese

   Cherry tomatoes
   (garnish)
   Parsley sprigs (garnish)

Carefully insert sharp knife into thickest part of side of each chicken breast. Make as long and deep an opening as possible without cutting through. (On some boned breasts it may be difficult to cut a uniform horizontal line; instead, use opening left where bone was removed.)

Melt 2 tablespoons butter in large skillet over medium-high heat. Add mushrooms and sauté 3 to 4 minutes. Stir in ham,

Sherry, lemon juice, tarragon and garlic and cook a few minutes more. Remove from heat and mix in cheese. Season to taste with salt and pepper. Stuff heaping tablespoon of mixture into each chicken breast. Place chicken on large baking sheet and cover with waxed paper. Place another baking sheet over chicken and put books or cans on top to weight chicken down. Refrigerate a few hours or preferably, overnight.

When ready to cook breasts, coat each lightly with flour, shaking off excess. Grease 9 × 13-inch baking dish. Melt ¼ cup butter in 12- to 14-inch skillet over medium-high heat and sauté chicken until deep golden brown on both sides and almost cooked through. Warm brandy, pour over chicken and flame. Transfer chicken to baking dish and set aside. Reserve skillet with pan juices.

Preheat oven to 350°F. Stir tomato paste and mustard into pan juices. Mix flour with small amount of chicken stock and blend until smooth. Stir in remaining stock, then add to skillet. Place over medium heat and simmer 5 minutes, stirring constantly with whisk until slightly thickened. Gradually add cream, stirring to blend well. Add wine, Sherry and white pepper. Pour over chicken, bake 15 minutes.

Melt ¼ cup butter in large skillet over medium-high heat. Add mushroom caps and artichoke bottoms and sauté briefly. Place one artichoke bottom, cup side up, on each breast and sprinkle with cheese. Bake 4 to 5 minutes, or until cheese is melted. Transfer chicken to heated platter. Place mushroom caps, fluted side up, on top of artichokes. Garnish with cherry tomatoes and parsley sprigs and serve.

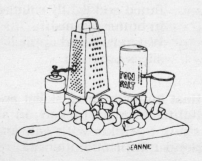

JEANNE

Chicken Normande

4 servings

- 5 tablespoons plus 1 teaspoon (⅔ stick) butter
- 1 3-pound chicken, cut into serving pieces
  Salt and freshly ground pepper
- ½ cup Calvados or applejack
- ½ cup chicken stock

- 2 tablespoons minced onion or shallot
- 1 large stalk celery, finely chopped
- 1 large green apple, peeled, cored and chopped

- 2 egg yolks
- ¾ cup whipping cream

- 8 medium mushrooms, fluted and lightly sautéed in butter (garnish)
  Watercress and apple slices (garnish)

Heat butter in large skillet and lightly brown chicken on all sides. Sprinkle with salt and pepper. Pour off butter and reserve. Remove pan from heat, pour heated Calvados over chicken and ignite, shaking pan to cover all parts. When flames die, add stock.

In another skillet sauté onion, celery and apple in reserved butter over medium heat until just soft. Add mixture to chicken and return chicken to medium heat. Bring to a boil, lower heat and simmer, covered, for about 20 minutes, or until chicken is tender. Transfer chicken pieces to heated platter and keep warm. Meanwhile, skim fat from skillet contents. Transfer contents to blender or processor and whirl until smooth. Return pureed vegetables and liquids to the same pan and cook over high heat, stirring occasionally, until about ⅔ cup remains. Remove from heat.

Beat egg yolks and cream together and gradually add to skillet contents. Return to low heat, stirring until sauce thickens to consistency of heavy cream. Coat chicken with sauce. Garnish with fluted mushrooms, watercress and apple slices.

Turkey

Perfect Roast Turkey with Dressing

20 to 25 servings

Butter or vegetable shortening
1 12- to 15-pound turkey, marinated and stuffed (see following recipes)

Preheat oven to 300°F. Place double-strength brown paper bag on counter seam side up. Cover bottom of inside of bag with butter or shortening. Fit marinated and stuffed turkey into bag, neck first and breast down. Secure bag with paper clips or staples. Set on a rack over a shallow roasting pan and place in preheated oven. Roast 20 to 25 minutes per pound. Do not open oven door until 30 minutes before turkey is done. At this point, take pan out of oven and poke small hole in bag under turkey breast so juices can run into pan. Remove bag and discard.

Turn turkey breast side up, place on rack and set it over another pan or cookie sheet. Pour juices from roasting pan into a bowl to be degreased for gravy. (If time allows, put drippings in freezer for about 30 minutes to allow excess grease to congeal for easy removal.) Return turkey to oven and roast 30 minutes longer, basting frequently with remaining marinade.

Finished turkey should reach 180° to 185°F when tested at thickest part of breast. If not using a thermometer, pierce the leg and note color of juice. If it is clear, the bird is done. (The oldest and still one of the best methods is to wiggle a drumstick. If it moves easily, the turkey is ready.) Remove pan from oven and set turkey on platter, covering lightly with foil to retain heat. Let stand 15 to 20 minutes before carving. (This makes carving easier.)

Marinade

Makes 1 cup

- 1 cup corn oil
- 1½ tablespoons Beau Monde seasoning
- 1½ tablespoons salt
- 2 tablespoons paprika
- ½ teaspoon freshly ground pepper
- 2 tablespoons minced fresh garlic

Blend all marinade ingredients. Use about half of marinade under skin of turkey and remaining marinade as basting liquid when turkey is roasting.

Clean turkey thoroughly. Starting from keel bone, lift turkey skin above breast with your fingers, carefully pushing skin away from the flesh. Try not to tear the skin and do not use a knife. Once skin is loosened, rub breast meat under skin with a generous amount of marinade. Then, starting at neck end, reach down under skin past breast and loosen skin around legs. Again, rub marinade between skin and meat. Rub inside cavity and outside skin with more marinade.

Cover loosely with plastic wrap and refrigerate until ready to stuff and roast.

Can be marinated and refrigerated up to 2 days before roasting.

Dressing

1 pound roll sausage
½ pound ground beef

½ cup (1 stick) butter
1 cup minced onion
2 garlic cloves, minced
1 cup minced celery
½ cup minced green bell pepper
½ pound sliced mushrooms

1 cup chicken stock
2 eggs, lightly beaten
1 teaspoon sage
1 8-ounce package cornbread stuffing mix
½ cup dry white wine
Salt and freshly ground pepper

Slice sausage ½ inch thick. Place in large skillet; cover with water and simmer until water is almost evaporated and fat is rendered from sausage. Discard any remaining liquid. Add beef and sauté until both meats are browned. Drain meat thoroughly on paper towels.

Melt butter in same skillet. Add onion and garlic; sauté until golden brown. Add celery, green pepper and mushrooms and cook 5 minutes.

Combine meats, vegetables and remaining ingredients. (The dressing should look moist; if not, add additional beaten egg.)

Fill cavity and neck of turkey with stuffing until about ¾ full, packing lightly. (Stuffing will expand during cooking.) Figure about ¾ cup stuffing per pound of turkey. Close with skewers or by sewing with needle and thread. For the neck, fold loose skin over and secure with skewers or thread.

Remaining dressing may be placed in baking dish and refrigerated until turkey is almost finished cooking. Bake 30 minutes or longer, covered or uncovered. Baste stuffing several times with roasting juices.

This stuffing is also good with chicken, crown roast of lamb and boned leg of lamb.

Double-Dressing Turkey

12 to 16 servings

> 1 12- to 15-pound turkey
> First Dressing (see following recipes)
> Second Dressing (see following recipes)
> Yorkshire Pudding (see following recipes)

Preheat oven to 300°F for turkey over 15 pounds or to 325°F for smaller bird.

Wash turkey thoroughly and prepare stuffings as directed below. Estimate 20 to 25 minutes of roasting time per pound.

Place stuffed turkey breast side down on Second Dressing in roasting pan. Roast for ½ of roasting time. Turn breast side up for remainder of time. Baste frequently with pan juices.

First Dressing

- 1 pound boned chicken
  breasts, skinned
- 2 egg whites
- ¼ cup whipping cream

- 1 cup mashed potatoes
- 8 diced slices egg bread,
  crusts removed

- 3 celery stalks and leaves,
  chopped
- 1 large onion, chopped
- 1 green bell pepper,
  seeded and chopped
- 3 large garlic cloves
- 6 fresh sage leaves or 1
  teaspoon dried
- 4 Jonathan apples, peeled,
  cored and chopped

- 1 tablespoon butter
- 3 tablespoons Calvados or
  applejack
  Pinch of freshly grated
  nutmeg
  Salt and freshly ground
  pepper

Chop chicken breasts in processor or meat grinder. Add egg whites and whipping cream.

Combine potatoes and bread in a large mixing bowl.

Puree celery, onion, green pepper, garlic, sage and apples in processor or blender.

Melt butter in a 10-inch saucepan and add pureed ingredients. Cook, stirring frequently, until thickened. Add Calvados. Combine with potato and chicken breast mixtures. Season with nutmeg, salt and pepper. Stuff turkey cavity ¾ full.

Second Dressing

- 4 diced slices egg bread, crusts removed
- 4 Jonathan apples, cored, peeled and sliced
- 1 10-ounce package frozen rhubarb, thawed and drained
- 1 large potato, peeled and thinly sliced
- 1 onion, coarsely chopped

Preheat oven to 325°F. Combine all ingredients. Place dressing in large roasting pan.

Yorkshire Pudding

- 4 eggs
- 1 cup all purpose flour
- 1 cup milk
  Pinch of salt

One-half hour before turkey is done, combine all ingredients for Yorkshire Pudding and beat thoroughly. Pour batter over Second Dressing. Return to oven for ½ hour or until pudding has absorbed all juices and is golden brown. Serve both dressings with each serving of turkey.

Game Birds

Spinach-Stuffed Cornish Game Hens

6 servings

    3 Cornish game hens
       Juice of 3 limes
 1½ teaspoons brandy
 1½ teaspoons olive oil
       Dried oregano

       Stuffing (see following recipe)
    1 teaspoon butter
 ½ cup chicken stock

Wash Cornish hens; dry with paper towels. Sprinkle lime juice into cavities. Mix brandy, oil and oregano in small saucepan and warm over low heat. Season cavities with this mixture. Flame twice to enhance flavor and burn off alcohol.

Lightly stuff hens and truss, securing legs and wings tightly to body. Brown in butter in skillet. Place in heavy 5-quart warmed casserole. Deglaze skillet with stock. Pour into casserole. Cover birds with parchment paper cut slightly larger than casserole. Make a small hole in paper to release steam. Cover casserole. Hens may be slowly simmered on top of range or baked in a 350°F oven for 1 hour (baste every 15 minutes). Remove cover of casserole during last 15 minutes of cooking.

Degrease sauce. Halve hens and place on an oval platter. Spoon sauce over hens or serve from separate bowl.

Stuffing

     1 teaspoon butter
     ½ cup chopped onion
     1 pound fresh spinach or
       1 10-ounce package
       frozen chopped, thawed

     3 Cornish game hen livers
     ½ cup ricotta cheese

1 ounce bacon, blanched
   and sautéed (optional)
1 teaspoon brandy
3 small crushed fresh
   oregano leaves or pinch
   of dried oregano
   Freshly grated nutmeg
   Tabasco sauce
   Salt and freshly ground
   pepper

Heat butter and sauté onion for
5 minutes. Mix in spinach and
cook until tender and dry, about
10 minutes. Transfer to bowl.

Chop livers finely; add to spinach with remaining ingredients.

Roast Stuffed Squab

These roasted squabs are
lovely accompanied with
braised endive and buttered
new potatoes.

6 servings

¾ cup fine breadcrumbs
½ cup beef stock
6 squab livers, sautéed in
   butter and coarsely
   chopped
3 cups mushrooms,
   coarsely chopped

¾ cup finely chopped fat
   salt pork
2 eggs, lightly beaten
2 small shallots, minced
2 tablespoons minced
   fresh parsley

6 squabs
6 slices bacon
¼ cup dry red wine
1 tablespoon cornstarch
2 tablespoons cold water

Figs and green and
purple grapes (garnish)

Preheat oven to 325°F. Soak
breadcrumbs in stock; press dry.
Mix together livers, mushrooms,
salt pork and breadcrumbs. Add
eggs, minced shallot and parsley and mix well.

Fill squab cavities with this mixture and close cavities by sewing or skewering. Place strip of
bacon over breast of each bird
and arrange in roasting pan.
Roast, basting frequently with
pan juices, for 40 minutes, or
until birds are tender and at desired degree of doneness. (Remove bacon during last 10
minutes to allow birds to brown

well.) Transfer birds to heated platter and keep warm.

Skim excess fat from pan juices and add wine, heating and stirring. Thicken with cornstarch mixed with water, if desired. Pour over birds and serve at once with garnish.

Honey-Glazed Ducklings

6 servings

> 3 4½-pound ducklings
>
> 2 medium onions, chopped
>
> 2 garlic cloves
>
> ¼ cup dark soy sauce
>
> ½ cup dry Sherry
>   Dash of Tabasco sauce
>
> ½ cup honey
>
> ½ teaspoon ground ginger
>
> ¼ teaspoon freshly ground black pepper
>
> Peel of 2 navel oranges
>
> Green grapes frosted with sugar (garnish)

For very crisp skin, hang ducks in a cool place (about 50°F) for 24 hours or longer (up to 4 days).

Snip off wing tips; wipe inside and out with paper towels. Preheat oven to 450°F. Whirl all remaining ingredients (except orange peel and grapes) in blender or processor until thoroughly liquefied. Place ducks breast side up on rack of oven with a pan below to catch drippings. Brush ducks generously with the honey mixture.

Place orange peel in the drip pan. Reduce heat to 350°F and roast ducks for 20 minutes per pound. Coat ducks with honey mixture every 10 to 15 minutes while roasting.

Garnish with sugar-frosted green grapes.

Roast Goose

The appearance of a goose, with its crackling golden skin guarding the succulent meat beneath, always signals a celebration. Yet many cooks shy away from goose, considering it difficult to cook and too fatty in the bargain. By carefully removing all the excess fat and roasting the goose at a low temperature, however, you won't have any problems. What's more, the rendered goose fat is a special dividend: It can be frozen and used later to give pâtés and terrines an exquisite flavor, and it's marvelous for sautéed potatoes.

8 servings

> 1 12- to 14-pound goose or 2 smaller geese, 6 to 7 pounds each
> 3 cups water
> 1 medium onion, sliced
> 1 large carrot
> 1 celery stalk with leaves
>   Salt
> 5 to 6 whole peppercorns
>
> 1 or 2 lemons, halved
>   Salt

Apple-Sage Dressing (see
following recipes)

Lemon–Red Currant
Glaze (see following
recipes)

Rendered goose fat or
butter

1 tablespoon butter
1 tablespoon all purpose
flour

Tangerine baskets filled
with chutney, sprigs of
watercress (garnish)

Remove neck and giblets from
goose, reserving liver, and place
in medium saucepan with water,
onion, carrot, celery, salt to taste
and peppercorns. Bring to boil,
then reduce heat and simmer
1½ hours, or until giblets are
tender. Allow to cool, then chop.

Remove all excess fat from goose
(render and reserve for future
use if desired). Rinse goose and
pat dry. Rub inside and out with
lemon halves and sprinkle cavities with salt.

Prepare Apple-Sage Dressing.

Preheat oven to 325°F. Lightly stuff body and neck cavities of goose, being sure not to pack too firmly, since dressing will expand during cooking. Place any extra dressing in a casserole to be heated with goose during last hour of cooking. Truss goose and skewer or sew opening. Place breast side up on rack in large roasting pan and roast 16 to 20 minutes per pound, or until thigh meat feels soft and joint moves easily. As goose cooks, remove rendered fat with bulb baster and set aside.

About 30 minutes before goose is done, paint with Lemon–Red Currant Glaze. When goose is done, transfer to warm platter and let stand 15 minutes.

Cut liver into 4 pieces and sauté in small amount of reserved rendered fat or butter until browned on outside but pink within. Chop for use in gravy.

Skim fat from roasting pan, add giblet stock and bring to boil over direct heat, scraping to remove browned bits from bottom of pan. Mix butter and flour together to form a paste (*beurre manié*) and add to stock. Season to taste with salt and pepper and stir in chopped giblets and liver.

Garnish platter with tangerine baskets filled with chutney and sprigs of watercress.

Apple-Sage Dressing

   6 tablespoons (¾ stick) butter
   1 cup chopped onion
   ½ cup chopped celery
   5 to 6 cups cubed bread
1½ cups peeled and diced tart apple
   1 cup ham, cut into ¼- to ½-inch cubes
   1 cup chopped walnuts
   ¼ cup chopped fresh parsley
   2 eggs, beaten
   1 teaspoon sage
   1 teaspoon salt
   ½ teaspoon dried thyme
   ½ teaspoon freshly ground pepper

Melt butter in medium skillet over medium-high heat. Add onion and celery and sauté until softened. Transfer to large bowl and mix in bread. Stir in remaining ingredients and blend well.

Lemon–Red Currant Glaze

Juice of 1 lemon
½ cup red currant jelly

Combine ingredients in small saucepan and heat until melted.

6

Seafood

Pompano en Papillote

6 servings

- ¼ cup (½ stick) butter
- ½ teaspoon minced garlic
- 1 tablespoon minced shallot
- 1 cup raw shrimp, shelled and deveined

- 2 tablespoons all purpose flour
- 1¾ cups concentrated fish stock
- 1 cup crabmeat

- 2 egg yolks
- ¼ cup dry white wine
  Salt and freshly ground pepper

6 6-ounce pompano,
   salmon, sea trout or
   sand dab fillets
½ cup minced fresh dill

6 lemon wedges (garnish)

In small skillet melt 2 tablespoons butter, add garlic and
shallot and sauté until translu-
cent. Add shrimp and sauté until just pink and barely cooked,
stirring constantly. Remove
shrimp, dice, and set aside.

Add remaining butter to skillet
and heat until bubbling. Add
flour and blend thoroughly. Remove from heat and add fish
stock. Mix thoroughly. Return to
heat and bring to a simmer, stirring constantly. Add reserved
shrimp and crabmeat.

Beat egg yolks with wine. Fold
into shrimp-crab mixture. Blend
thoroughly. Season with salt and
pepper. Chill until very thick.

Butter six 18-inch squares of
heavy-duty aluminum foil. Place
a fish fillet on each square. Coat
with shrimp-crab mixture;
sprinkle with dill. Bring edges of
foil together and twist. Place on

a hot grill and cook, using 10
minutes per inch as a time measure. Place packets on heated
plates and serve garnished with
lemon wedges.

Stuffed Salmon

8 servings

5 pounds whole fresh
  salmon, cleaned, head
  and tail left on
2 tablespoons fresh lemon
  juice
2 tablespoons dry white
  wine
  Salt and freshly ground
  pepper

¼ cup (½ stick) butter
1 large onion, finely
  chopped
2 stalks celery with leaves,
  finely chopped
½ cup minced fresh
  parsley
1½ pounds mushrooms,
  thinly sliced
2 teaspoons minced fresh
  dill

Salt and freshly ground
pepper

Parsley Butter (see
following recipe)

Wash fish and pat dry inside and
outside with paper towels. Make
2 slashing incisions on each side
of fish. Rub inside of fish with
lemon juice and wine. Dust with
salt and pepper.

Melt butter in frying pan; add
onion and celery and sauté until golden brown. Add parsley
and mushrooms. Sauté 3 to 5
minutes. Add minced dill and
salt and pepper.

Stuff fish with mushroom filling.
Close opening with metal stuffing skewers. Brush fish with
Parsley Butter. Place on well-
oiled hinged oblong fish grill
over medium heat, using 10
minutes per inch as a time measure. Turn fish once, basting frequently. Serve with additional
Parsley Butter.

*White fish or striped bass may
be prepared in the same manner.*

Parsley Butter

Makes 1 cup

    1 cup (2 sticks) butter
    ¼ cup minced fresh
       parsley
    2 tablespoons lemon juice
       or to taste
       Freshly ground black
       pepper

Cream butter and add remaining ingredients. Mix thoroughly.

Turban of Sole

6 to 8 servings

Enriched Béchamel Sauce
    3 tablespoons butter
    2 shallots or white part of
       1 green onion, minced
    5 tablespoons all purpose
       flour
    1 cup milk, room
       temperature

    4 egg yolks
       Salt and freshly ground
       pepper

Spinach Mousse

> 1 10-ounce package frozen
> chopped spinach,
> thawed and well drained
> 1 tablespoon minced green
> onion tops
> ½ teaspoon freshly grated
> nutmeg
> 2 egg whites
> Pinch of salt
> Pinch of cream of tartar
> Salt and freshly ground
> pepper

Salmon Mousse

> 1 pound fresh salmon,
> filleted and ground
> 1 tablespoon fresh minced
> dill or 1½ teaspoons
> dried dillweed
> 1 teaspoon fresh lemon
> juice
> 1 teaspoon paprika
> 2 egg whites
> Pinch of salt
> Pinch of cream of tartar

> 8 or 9 sole fillets

> Sauce Beurre Blanc (see
> following recipe)

For béchamel: Melt butter in 1-quart saucepan. Add shallot and sauté until lightly browned. Blend in flour, stirring well. Remove from heat. Gradually add milk, whisking to blend. Cook over low heat, stirring frequently until thickened. Remove from heat.

Beat yolks in small bowl. Carefully blend in a bit of the hot sauce. Add yolk mixture to saucepan, blending well, and return to heat about 1 minute. Add salt and pepper to taste.

For Spinach Mousse: Combine spinach and half the béchamel with the onion tops and nutmeg. Beat egg whites until foamy. Add salt and cream of tartar and continue beating until stiff but not dry. Fold into spinach mixture. Add salt and pepper to taste. Set aside.

For Salmon Mousse: Combine salmon, remaining béchamel, dill, lemon juice and paprika. Beat egg whites until foamy. Add salt and cream of tartar and continue beating until stiff but not dry. Fold into salmon mixture. Set aside.

Preheat oven to 350°F. Rinse sole in salted water. Flatten fillets slightly with a moistened mallet or rolling pin.

In a well-buttered 8- or 9-cup ring mold, arrange fillets skinned (darker) side up and slightly overlapping. Allow small end of each fillet to hang over center of mold and wide end to extend over outside edge. Spread spinach mousse carefully on top of fillets. Spread salmon mousse over spinach. Fold edges back over. Cover mold with buttered waxed paper.

Place ring mold in *bain-marie* (a roasting pan half filled with boiling water works well) and bake 40 to 45 minutes. Pour off all liquid. After 5 minutes, turn out onto platter, blotting up any excess liquid to prevent sauce from being diluted. Serve with Sauce Beurre Blanc.

The center of the mold may be filled with mushrooms lightly sautéed with minced shallot and sprinkled with parsley.

Enriched Béchamel Sauce may be prepared 4 days ahead. It also freezes well.

Spinach Mousse may also be served as a vegetable side dish, or placed between buttered fish fillets, covered with buttered waxed paper and baked at 350°F until fish flakes easily (time will depend on size of fillets). Serve with Sauce Beurre Blanc or homemade hollandaise.

Sauce Beurre Blanc l'Ermitage

Makes 1 cup

- 2 tablespoons (¼ stick) butter
- 2 shallots, finely minced
- ⅓ cup dry white wine
- 2 tablespoons white wine vinegar
- 2 tablespoons whipping cream
- 2 whole parsley stems

- 1 cup (2 sticks) unsalted butter, chilled and cut into ½-inch cubes
  Salt and freshly ground pepper

Melt 2 tablespoons butter in 1½-quart nonaluminum saucepan. Add shallots and cook until transparent but not colored. Blend in wine and vinegar and cook until reduced to 1 tablespoon. Add cream and parsley stems and allow to boil gently 2 to 3 minutes. Remove parsley.

Over very low heat, beat butter into sauce piece by piece, whisking constantly. As each piece is almost creamed into sauce, add next piece. The sauce will be thick (the consistency of light hollandaise) and ivory colored. Add salt and pepper to taste. Strain.

May be made ½ hour ahead and held over warm water. Also excellent with plain poached fish.

Roquefort-and-Shrimp-Stuffed Sole

8 servings

- 1 cup (2 sticks) butter, softened
- 4 ounces cream cheese, room temperature
- 6 ounces uncooked shrimp, cut into small pieces
- 3 to 6 ounces Roquefort cheese
- 2 tablespoons fresh lemon juice
- 2 teaspoons anise liqueur (optional)
- 1 teaspoon chopped fresh parsley
- 1 teaspoon chopped chives
- 1 green onion, minced
- ⅛ teaspoon hot pepper sauce
- ⅛ teaspoon Worcestershire sauce
  Freshly ground pepper to taste
  Salt (optional)
- 8 10-ounce sole fillets*

*If 10-ounce fillets are unavailable, use several 5- to 6-ounce pieces. Overlap them when rolling to make a thicker fillet.

2 eggs, beaten
Breadcrumbs
½ cup (1 stick) butter,
melted

Sautéed mushrooms
(optional)

Combine first 12 ingredients in
mixing bowl and blend thoroughly. Taste before adding salt,
since Roquefort is salty. Refrigerate at least 20 minutes.

Preheat oven to 375°F. Pat fish
dry. Spread about ¼ cup of
chilled filling on skin side
(darker side) of each fillet. Roll
fillets about halfway. Carefully
fold in outer edges to hold mixture inside. Complete rolling.

Dip each fillet into beaten egg
and roll in crumbs. Place in
shallow buttered baking dish
just large enough to hold fillets.
(If preferred, place rolled fillets
in buttered baking dish without
dipping in egg and bread-
crumbs.) Top with remaining
filling (if any) and drizzle with
melted butter.

Bake approximately 20 minutes,
or until sole is white and flaky

but *not* dry and crumbly. *Do not overcook.* Check frequently after 15 minutes. Top with sautéed mushrooms just before serving, if desired.

Sole with Shrimp Sauce

The beauty of this dish is that it calls for no last-minute preparation. Everything is done ahead so the host or hostess can join the guests while the first course warms in the oven.

8 servings

- 6 to 8 ounces fish trimmings
- ½ cup water
- ½ cup dry white wine
- ½ medium onion, sliced
- ½ carrot, sliced
- 1 small celery stalk with leaves
- 1 tablespoon fresh lemon juice
- ¼ teaspoon sugar
- 8 small (3- to 4-ounce) sole fillets
  Salt

3 tablespoons butter

2 tablespoons all purpose flour

⅓ cup whipping cream
Salt and freshly ground white pepper

1 pound cooked small or medium shrimp

Combine first 8 ingredients with salt and pepper to taste in medium saucepan. Place over high heat and bring to boil; reduce heat and simmer 30 minutes. Strain stock and set aside.

Preheat oven to 400°F. Fold each fish fillet crosswise in thirds, as if folding a letter, and place in baking dish large enough to hold all fillets in single layer. Sprinkle lightly with salt and pour reserved stock over. Cover and bake 10 minutes.

Transfer fish to individual oven-proof gratin dishes, reserving cooking liquid. Cover and refrigerate.

Melt butter in skillet over medium heat. Stir in flour. Remove from heat and gradually stir in 1 cup reserved cooking liquid. Return to heat and cook until thickened. Add cream and season to taste with salt and pepper. Remove from heat and stir in shrimp. Spoon sauce over fish, cover and return to refrigerator.

When ready to serve, preheat oven to 400°F. Bake fish uncovered 10 minutes, or until sauce bubbles and fish is completely heated through.

Fish Flambé with Fennel

6 servings

- ¼ cup olive oil
- 1 teaspoon dried fennel
- 1 teaspoon dried thyme
- 2 tablespoons minced fresh parsley
- 2 tablespoons dry white wine or fresh lemon juice
- 1 tablespoon anise liqueur
- 1 3-pound bluefish, striped bass or perch, or six 10-ounce trout
- 2 tablespoons Cognac

Combine olive oil, fennel, thyme, parsley, wine and liqueur. Make

2 slanting incisions on each side of fish. Let fish marinate while preparing barbecue grill.

Broil fish over medium-hot coals, using 10 minutes per inch as a time measure, turning once, brushing occasionally with marinade. Place on hot platter.

Heat Cognac and flame, then pour over fish. Serve with natural juices on the platter.

Shrimp Kiev

6 servings

- ¾ cup (1½ sticks) unsalted butter, softened
- 3 medium garlic cloves *or* shallots, minced
- 18 to 21 uncooked jumbo shrimp, shelled and deveined
- ⅓ cup dry white wine
- 5 tablespoons fresh lemon juice
- 3 tablespoons minced fresh parsley
- ¾ teaspoon salt
- ¼ teaspoon freshly ground white pepper

    3 eggs, beaten
 1½ tablespoons oil
    1 cup all purpose flour

    1 cup breadcrumbs

      Shortening or oil for
      deep frying

      Mustard Hollandaise
      Sauce (see following
      recipe)
      Lemon wedges and
      parsley (garnish)

Combine butter and garlic in small bowl and mix thoroughly. Chill well. Quickly shape into 18 to 21 tiny rolls about ¼ inch in diameter. Place on waxed paper and freeze.

Butterfly shrimp by slitting lengthwise on the inside curve, making sure not to cut all the way through. Sprinkle a piece of waxed paper with a little wine and lay shrimp out flat (like an open book). Cover with another sheet of waxed paper and pound shrimp flat, using mallet or flat side of cleaver and being careful not to tear flesh. Brush shrimp with remaining wine and place frozen butter roll on each.

Sprinkle with lemon juice, parsley, salt and pepper.

Combine eggs and oil in small bowl. Starting with long side, roll shrimp around butter, tucking in ends (shrimp are gelatinous and will stick together). Coat each with flour, shaking off excess. Dip shrimp into egg-oil mixture.

Add remaining flour to breadcrumbs. Roll shrimp in flour-crumb mixture, carefully coating ends of rolls. Place shrimp seam side down on baking sheet and freeze at least ½ hour, or refrigerate at least 1 hour, until shrimp are thoroughly chilled.

Heat shortening in electric skillet, deep heavy saucepan or deep fryer to 375°F. Fry shrimp a few at a time, allowing about 3 minutes if from refrigerator or about 5 or 6 minutes if from freezer. Remove with slotted spoon and drain on paper towels. Serve hot with Mustard Hollandaise Sauce and garnish with lemon and parsley.

Shrimp rolls may be assembled, wrapped and frozen for up to 4 weeks; do not thaw before frying.

Mustard Hollandaise Sauce

4 egg yolks
2 tablespoons fresh lemon juice
1 tablespoon Dijon mustard
½ cup (1 stick) butter, heated
2 tablespoons boiling water
½ teaspoon salt
Ground red pepper

Combine yolks, lemon juice and mustard in blender (*do not use processor*) and blend 30 seconds. Pour in sizzling hot butter and boiling water and blend until thickened. Stir in salt and red pepper. If sauce is too thick, thin with additional lemon juice or boiling water.

This sauce may be placed in a preheated vacuum bottle and held at room temperature up to 1 hour before serving.

Index

Credits

The following people contributed the recipes included in this book:

Mary Dorra
Robert Ehrman and Ray Henderson
Marie-Odile Fazzolare and Nancy
  Brehm
Karen Gregorakis
Zack Hanle
Isobel Robins Konecky
Rita Leinwand
Joan McCormick
Jinx and Jefferson Morgan
Ronald S. Wirth
Janet and Roger Yaseen